W9-ABW-606

THE BIG BITE
BOOK OF
PIZZAS

THE BIG BITE BOOK OF PIZZAS

MEG JANSZ

SMITHMARK

This edition published in 1994 by
SMITHMARK Publishers Inc.,
16 East 32nd Street,
New York, NY 10016.

1 2 3 4 5 6 7 8 9

SMITHMARK books are available for bulk purchase
for sales promotion and premium use. For details
write or call the manager of special sales,
SMITHMARK Publishers Inc.,
16 East 32nd Street, New York,
NY 10016; (212) 532-6600.

ISBN: 0-8317-0716-X

Printed in Singapore.

CREDITS

Author and home economist: Meg Jansz
Home economist's assistants: Nicole
    Szabason and Cara Hobday
Managing editor: Lisa Dyer
Photographer: Ken Field
Designer: Paul Johnson
Stylist: Marian Price
Copy editor: Alison Leach
Filmset: SX Composing Ltd, England
Color Separation: P&W Graphics Pte, Ltd,
    Singapore

7.98

CONTENTS

INTRODUCTION   6

PIZZA BASES & SAUCES   10

THIN-CRUST PIZZAS   18

DEEP-PAN PIZZAS   36

CALZONES & SFINCIONES   50

SPECIALTY PIZZAS   64

INDEX   80

INTRODUCTION

The Big Bite Book of Pizzas explores pizza-making in its widest sense, from standard thin-crust and deep-pan pizzas through calzones and sfinciones to specialty pizzas made from unusual bases. Some of the recipes in the book are familiar favorites, while others are exciting new innovations, inspired by international cuisines.

In Italian the word 'pizza' means pie, so the term 'pizza pie' is really a repetition of the same word. The pizza was first brought from Italy to America in 1905 by Gennaro Lombardi, who opened the first pizzeria in New York. His version of the pizza pie from Naples is now international food and the world would be unhappy without it!

PIZZA DOUGH

To make your own pizza dough, always use "strong" flour or bread flour, as this has a high gluten content which allows the yeast to raise the dough to its maximum point. Rapid-rise dried yeast is used in all the recipes in this book because it is so simple to handle, and can be stored long-term in your kitchen cupboard. When making deep-pan pizza dough, the rapid-rise dried yeast can be increased to 1 tablespoon in any of the four dough recipes on page 10. This will create an even lighter dough.

KNEADING

To knead by hand, place the prepared dough ball on a lightly floured surface and, with floured hands, press down on the dough with the heel of your hands and push it away from you. Fold the pressed dough back over itself, and repeat, turning the dough around a little

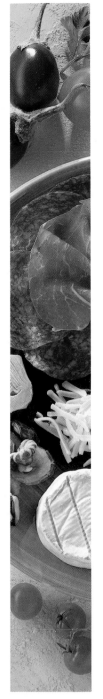

each time until you have completed a full circle. Always make sure you have enough flour on the work surface and on your hands to prevent the dough sticking. Kneading will take 10-15 minutes, and the dough is ready when it is smooth in texture, and elastic and springy to the touch. Do not overknead.

If you have an electric mixer with a dough hook, you can knead the dough this way, but be careful to stop kneading as soon as it is springy. It is easy to overwork dough with an electric mixer. Kneading by this method will take only 8-10 minutes.

STORING DOUGH

Pizza dough may be stored in the refrigerator for up to 2 days, sealed in a lightly oiled plastic bag and then used as suggested in the recipes. Alternatively, the dough can be frozen for up to 3 months if wrapped in plastic wrap or in plastic bags and sealed in an airtight box. Thaw the dough for a few hours at room temperature before using.

PREPARING THIN-CRUST BASES

To shape a thin-crust pizza base by rolling, place the ball of dough on a lightly floured surface and roll it out with a floured rolling pin to produce a flat disk. Continue rolling the dough to produce a thin circle about ¼ inch thick. Place the circle on a baking sheet dusted with cornmeal, and continue as described in the recipe. Cornmeal on the baking sheets pro-

RIGHT: Choose the freshest ingredients possible from supermarkets and specialty stores for your pizza creations.

duces a crisp base. If you like thin bases, but prefer them to be not too crispy, roll the dough out to about ½ inch thick.

Thin-crust bases can also be made by stretching the dough. Place the ball of dough on a lightly floured surface and shape it into a flat disk with floured hands. Then press out from the center of the dough to produce a circle. When it has nearly reached its desired thickness, place one hand on the center of the dough circle, and gently stretch it with the other hand to form the finished circle.

PREPARING DEEP-PAN BASES

Deep-pan pizza cases generally have a rim to contain the filling. To shape the bases, place a ball of dough on a lightly floured work surface and roll it out until it is about ½-¾ inch thick. Roll out so the dough is about 1 inch larger all around than the base of the pizza pan. Place the circle of dough in the pan, and pull the edges of the dough up around the sides of the pan to create the rim. Smooth out the base with the heel of your hands. Then let the dough base rise as described in the individual recipes before continuing. If you prefer a thinner crusted deep-pan pizza, do not let the prepared base rise, but fill and cook the pizza as quickly as possible.

PIZZA SAUCES

Although a tomato-based sauce is the most popular, many other recipes can be used. All sauces, however, need to be fairly thick so they will stay on the base. Sauces can be made ahead of time and stored in the refrigerator for 4-5 days. The fresh pestos on page 16 will stay fresh for up to 2 weeks in the refrigerator provided they are covered with a layer of oil.

CHEESE TOPPING

Cheese is very popular on pizzas, but is not essential to produce a wonderful-tasting pizza. If you dislike cheese or are calorie-counting, leave cheese out of the recipe and use more sauce or other toppings.

A good melting cheese is essential for pizza, and cheese should be grated, crumbled or thinly sliced, so it melts and spreads evenly. Mozzarella is a classic pizza cheese, and you can also buy hard mozzarella which is easy to grate. Soft cheeses make good base cheeses for sauce-less pizzas as they spread easily.

EQUIPMENT

Good pizzas can be made at home with very simple equipment. Apart from mixing bowls and rolling pins, the only essential equipment are baking sheets and pans.

In this book, all the thin-crust pizzas, calzones and sfiniciones have been made using heavy baking sheets dusted with cornmeal. If you are a frequent pizza maker, a baking stone would be a useful piece of equipment to own. The stone needs to be thoroughly heated in the oven before the uncooked pizza is placed directly on it and baked. Pizza peels are long-handled paddle-like utensils which are useful for transporting pizzas to the baking stone.

Deep-pan pizzas should be made in pizza pans. A heavy pizza pan made from black steel is an advantage, as it will hold heat and withstand high oven temperatures without warping. However, a good-quality, oiled baking pan will also produce successful results.

RIGHT: Wonderfully tasty pizzas can be made easily without any special equipment.

PIZZA BASES & SAUCES

Homemade dough bases are actually very easy to prepare and will enable you to use unusual bases that cannot be bought. Sauces also play a vital part in good pizzas. Choose from one of the three tomato-based sauces or try Roasted Pepper Sauce for a rich, Mediterranean flavor. Corn Sauce is excellent with chicken and seafood.

BASIC PIZZA DOUGH

3 cups strong white bread flour
I teaspoon salt
2¼ teaspoons rapid-rise dried yeast
I tablespoon olive oil
I cup lukewarm water

Sift the flour, salt and yeast into a large mixing bowl. Make a well in the center, and pour in the oil and water. Stir thoroughly, gradually drawing in all the flour to form a soft dough.

Knead the dough by hand, on a well-floured surface, for 12-15 minutes until it is smooth, elastic and shiny.

Place the kneaded dough in an oiled bowl, turning the dough ball around until it is completely covered in oil. Cover the bowl with plastic wrap, and leave to rise in a warm place for 1½-2 hours until it has doubled in size.

Turn the dough onto a floured surface, knock it down, and knead again briefly for about 30 seconds. Roll out and use as required.

Variation: Add 2 tablespoons freshly chopped herbs of your choice to the flour, salt and yeast at the beginning of the recipe.

CLOCKWISE: Cornmeal Pizza Dough, Herby Basic Pizza Dough, Whole-wheat Pizza Dough

CORNMEAL PIZZA DOUGH

2 cups strong white bread flour
I teaspoon salt
2¼ teaspoons rapid-rise dried yeast
I cup coarse cornmeal
I tablespoon olive oil
I cup lukewarm water

Sift the flour, salt and yeast into a large mixing bowl, then stir in the cornmeal. To finish, follow the Basic Pizza Dough recipe.

WHOLE-WHEAT PIZZA DOUGH

1¼ cups strong white bread flour
1⅓ cups strong whole-wheat bread flour
I tablespoon salt
2¼ teaspoons rapid-rise dried yeast
I tablespoon vegetable oil
I cup lukewarm water

Sift the two flours, salt and yeast into a large bowl. To finish, follow the Basic Pizza Dough recipe.

RICH PIZZA DOUGH

2 cups strong white bread flour
I tablespoon salt
2¼ teaspoons rapid-rise dried yeast
5 tablespoons lukewarm milk
3 tablespoons melted unsalted butter
I beaten egg

Sift the flour, salt and yeast into a large bowl. Make a well in the center and pour in the milk, butter and egg. To finish, follow the Basic Pizza Dough recipe.

BASIC TOMATO SAUCE

3½ cups canned chopped tomatoes
3 tablespoons olive oil
2 cloves garlic, crushed
½ teaspoon superfine sugar
Grated zest of ½ lemon
Salt and ground black pepper
2 tablespoons chopped fresh parsley

Place the chopped tomatoes, olive oil, garlic, sugar, lemon zest and seasoning in a saucepan. Bring to a boil, then reduce the heat, and simmer, uncovered, for 40-50 minutes until the sauce is thick and pulpy. Stir in the chopped parsley and taste; adjust seasoning if necessary.

Let the sauce cool. If you prefer a smoother sauce, purée the cooled mixture in a food processor. Store the sauce in the refrigerator, and use as required. It will keep fresh for 3-4 days.

MAKES ABOUT 2½ CUPS

FRESH TOMATO & HERB SAUCE

2 pounds ripe plum tomatoes
1 medium onion
2 tablespoons chopped celery leaves
1 tablespoon brown sugar
Salt and ground black pepper
⅔ cup red wine
2 tablespoons chopped fresh herbs of your choice, such as oregano, parsley or basil

Chop the tomatoes roughly, and place them in a heavy-bottomed saucepan. Chop the onion finely, and add this to the pan, along with the celery leaves, sugar, seasoning and red wine. Cover and simmer the tomato mixture for 15 minutes. Uncover the pan, stir the tomato mixture, and simmer for a further 40 minutes. Let the mixture cool, then purée it in a blender until the sauce is thick and smooth. Stir in the fresh herbs and taste; adjust seasoning if necessary.

Store the sauce in the refrigerator, and use as required to top pizza bases, or to serve with calzone. It will keep fresh for 4-5 days. Alternatively, freeze the sauce in small quantities and defrost when needed.

MAKES ABOUT 3¾ CUPS

TOP: Basic Tomato Sauce
BOTTOM: Fresh Tomato & Herb Sauce

TOMATO & CHILI SAUCE

2 pounds ripe tomatoes
3 cloves garlic, unpeeled
3 tablespoons olive oil
3-4 fresh red chilies, seeded and finely chopped
2 shallots, finely chopped
1 teaspoon superfine sugar
Salt and ground black pepper

Preheat the broiler to hot. Broil the tomatoes for 12 minutes, turning occasionally, until they soften and the skins begin to become charred. Remove, and let cool. Broil the garlic cloves for 10 minutes, until they are browned and softened. Remove, and let cool, then peel off the skins and mash the garlic. Do not peel the tomatoes, just chop them roughly.

Heat the oil in a saucepan, and add the chilies and shallots. Cook for 5 minutes, then stir in the tomatoes, garlic, sugar and seasoning. Simmer, uncovered, for 15 minutes until the sauce is thick. Let the sauce cool, then purée it in a blender until smooth. Taste and adjust seasoning if necessary.

Store the sauce in the refrigerator, and use as required to top pizza bases, or to serve with calzone. It will keep fresh for 4-5 days. Alternatively, freeze the sauce in small quantities, and defrost when needed.

MAKES ABOUT 3¾ CUPS

ROASTED PEPPER SAUCE

3 red bell peppers
3 orange bell peppers
3 tablespoons olive oil
4 shallots, chopped
2 cloves garlic, crushed
1¼ cups vegetable stock
1 tablespoon red wine vinegar
1 tablespoon superfine sugar
Salt and ground black pepper

Halve the peppers lengthwise, and remove the cores and seeds. Place them skin-side up on a baking sheet and cook under a preheated hot broiler for 10-12 minutes, until the skins begin to blacken and blister. Let the grilled peppers cool, then skin them and chop coarsely.

Heat the oil in a pan, and sauté the shallots and garlic for 4-5 minutes until softened. Add the skinned, chopped bell peppers, the stock, vinegar, sugar and seasoning, and cook the mixture, uncovered, for 10-15 minutes until the liquid has reduced slightly.

Let the mixture cool, and then purée it to produce a smooth, thick sauce. Taste and adjust seasoning if necessary. Store the sauce in the refrigerator, and use as required. It will keep fresh for 4-5 days.

MAKES ABOUT 3 CUPS

TOP: Roasted Pepper Sauce
BOTTOM: Tomato & Chili Sauce

CORN SAUCE

¼ cup butter
1 onion, chopped
3 cloves garlic, crushed
2¼ cups canned corn kernels, drained
1¼ cups vegetable stock
⅔ cup heavy cream
Salt and ground black pepper
2 tablespoons lemon juice
1 teaspoon superfine sugar
2 tablespoons chopped fresh parsley

Melt the butter in a saucepan, and sauté the onion and garlic for 5 minutes until soft. Reserve 4 tablespoons of the corn, and add the rest to the onion mixture. Stir in the stock, and cook the mixture over a high heat for 10 minutes, until the liquid has reduced slightly. Add the cream and seasoning, and boil the sauce for 10-15 minutes to reduce it further. When reduced, stir in the lemon juice and sugar.

Let the sauce cool, then purée it in a food processor until smooth. Stir in the parsley and reserved corn; taste and adjust seasoning if necessary.

Store the sauce in the refrigerator, and use as required. It will keep well for 4-5 days.

MAKES ABOUT 2½ CUPS

FRESH PARSLEY PESTO

1½ cups chopped fresh parsley
2 cloves garlic, crushed
⅓ cup toasted pine nuts
⅓ cup toasted, slivered almonds
Generous ½ cup grated Parmesan cheese
Salt and ground black pepper
⅔ cup extra virgin olive oil

Place all the ingredients except the olive oil in a food processor. Process until well combined and paste-like. Drizzle ½ cup of the olive oil into the paste in a thin stream, until it is well combined; a smooth, thick pesto sauce should be produced.

Spoon the pesto into a bowl or jar, and pour the remaining olive oil over it, then cover and store in the refrigerator. It will keep well for up to 2 weeks. Use as required.

MAKES ABOUT 1½ CUPS

FRESH BASIL PESTO

2 cups chopped fresh basil leaves
3 cloves garlic, crushed
¾ cup toasted pine nuts
Generous ½ cup grated Parmesan cheese
Salt and ground black pepper
½ cup extra virgin olive oil

Prepare basil pesto following the method for Parsley Pesto above. Use 6 tablespoons of the olive oil to make the pesto, and the remaining 2 tablespoons of oil to cover the pesto. Use as required.

MAKES ABOUT 1¾ CUPS

COUNTER CLOCKWISE: Fresh Basil Pesto, Fresh Parsley Pesto, Corn Sauce

THIN-CRUST PIZZAS

This chapter includes thin, crispy pizzas to suit every taste. Most of the recipes make two large pizzas which would serve two people as a main meal or four as a snack. Sun-dried Tomato Pizza and Pesto, Tomato & Garlic Pizza make four smaller pizzas suitable for light lunches.

SUN-DRIED TOMATO PIZZA

Basic Pizza Dough (see page 10)
Cornmeal for dusting
4 tablespoons olive oil
1½ cups Fresh Tomato & Herb Sauce (see page 12)
8 ounces mozzarella cheese
12 halves of sun-dried tomato in oil
16 green olives
4 teaspoons chopped fresh oregano

Prepare the dough. When it is ready for use, divide it into four equal portions. Roll out or stretch pizza dough as described on page 6. Make four 8-inch thin-crust pizza bases. Place the bases on baking sheets lightly dusted with cornmeal, and brush them all over with 2 tablespoons of the olive oil.

Spread 6 tablespoons of the sauce over each pizza base, leaving a ½-inch border. Slice the mozzarella and divide it between the pizzas. Cut the sun-dried tomatoes into thick slices, and scatter them over the pizzas, along with the olives. Drizzle the remaining oil over the pizzas.

Bake the pizzas, in batches, in a preheated oven at 475°F for 12-15 minutes, until the crusts are golden. Remove, sprinkle with oregano, and serve at once.

MAKES FOUR 8-INCH PIZZAS

PIZZA MARGHERITA

Basic Pizza Dough (see page 10)
Cornmeal for dusting
4 tablespoons olive oil
¾ cup Basic Tomato Sauce (see page 12)
1 cup grated hard mozzarella cheese
16 cherry tomatoes, halved
16 small black olives
Salt and ground black pepper
Several fresh basil leaves

Prepare the dough. When it is ready to use, divide it into two equal portions. Roll out or stretch pizza dough as described on page 6. Make two 10-inch thin-crust pizza bases. Place the bases on baking sheets lighly dusted with cornmeal. Prick the centers of each base several times with a fork, and brush them all over with half the olive oil.

Spread half the tomato sauce over each base to within ½ inch of the edges. Scatter the cheese over each pizza.

Divide the halved tomatoes and the black olives between the two pizzas. Season with salt and ground black pepper, and drizzle the remaining olive oil over each pizza.

Bake the pizzas in a preheated oven at 475°F for 12-15 minutes, until the crusts are golden and the cheese has melted. Remove from the oven, scatter some fresh basil over each pizza, and serve at once.

MAKES TWO 10-INCH PIZZAS

RIGHT: Pizza Margherita

PIZZA TRE PEPPERONI

Rich Pizza Dough (see page 10)
1 red bell pepper
1 orange bell pepper
1 yellow bell pepper
Cornmeal for dusting
4 tablespoons olive oil
2 cloves garlic, crushed
¾ cup Tomato & Chili Sauce (see page 14)
Salt and ground black pepper
2 teaspoons chopped fresh parsley

Prepare the dough. While waiting for the dough to rise, prepare the broiled bell peppers. Halve the peppers, and remove the core and seeds. Place them, cut-side down, on a baking sheet and broil for about 10 minutes, until the skins begin to blacken. Place the peppers in a plastic bag and let cool. When cool, remove the skins, and slice the peppers into thick strips.

When the dough is ready for use, divide it into two equal portions. Roll out or stretch the pizza dough as described on page 6. Make two 10-inch thin-crust pizza bases. Place bases on baking sheets lightly dusted with cornmeal, prick the center of each base with the prongs of a fork, and brush with 3 tablepoons of the olive oil mixed with the garlic.

Spread the sauce over the two bases, leaving a ½-inch border. Scatter the mixed pepper strips over the pizzas, and season. Drizzle the remaining olive oil over the pizzas.

Bake the pizzas in a preheated oven at 475°F for 10-12 minutes. Remove from the oven, scatter with the parsley, and serve at once.

MAKES TWO 10-INCH PIZZAS

ROASTED GARLIC & EGGPLANT PIZZA

Basic Pizza Dough (see page 10)
1 medium eggplant, sliced into 10 circles
4 cloves garlic, peeled and thickly sliced
Olive oil for brushing
Cornmeal for dusting
3 ounces creamy goat cheese
2 tablespoons sun-dried tomato paste
4 ounces goat cheese with rind
Salt and ground black pepper
2 teaspoons torn Italian flat-leafed parsley

Prepare the dough. While waiting for the dough to rise, place the eggplant and garlic slices on a baking sheet, and brush with olive oil. Cook the garlic in a preheated oven at 400°F for 4-5 minutes and the eggplant for 8-9 minutes. Let cool.

When the dough is ready for use, divide it into two equal portions. Roll out or stretch the pizza dough as described on page 6. Make two 10-inch thin-crust pizza bases. Place bases on baking sheets lightly dusted with cornmeal, and brush with olive oil.

Mix together the soft, creamy goat cheese and the sun-dried tomato paste. Spread over the two bases, leaving a ½-inch border. Slice the goat cheese with rind into eight thin circles, and place four on each pizza. Divide the eggplant and garlic between the pizzas, season, and drizzle with olive oil.

Bake the pizzas in a preheated oven at 475°F for 12-15 minutes. Sprinkle with parsley, and serve at once.

MAKES TWO 10-INCH PIZZAS

LEFT: Pizza Tre Pepperoni
RIGHT: Roasted Garlic & Eggplant Pizza

PIZZA FRUTTI DI MARE

2 purchased 9-inch thin-crust pizza bases
Cornmeal for dusting
4 tablespoons olive oil
3 tablespoons chopped fresh mixed herbs, such as
parsley, chives and chervil
⅓ cup smooth cottage cheese
2 tablespoons milk
Salt and ground black pepper
I cup grated Emmental cheese
12 ounces frozen fruits de mer (mixed seafood),
defrosted and well drained
3 tablespoons grated Parmesan cheese
I tablespoons fresh chervil leaves

Place the pizza bases on baking sheets lightly dusted with cornmeal. Mix together 3 tablespoons of the olive oil with the chopped mixed herbs, and brush this over the pizza bases.

Mix together the cottage cheese, milk and seasoning, and spread this mixture over the two bases, leaving a ½-inch border around the edges. Scatter the grated Emmental over the pizzas, and divide the seafood between the pizzas. Sprinkle on the Parmesan cheese, grind some salt and pepper on top, and drizzle the remaining olive oil over the pizzas.

Bake the pizzas in a preheated oven at 425°F for 12-14 minutes, until the crusts are crisp and golden and the cheese has melted. Remove from the oven, scatter with chervil, and serve immediately.

MAKES TWO 9-INCH PIZZAS

ANCHOVY, BROCCOLI & PINE NUT PIZZA

Whole-wheat Pizza Dough (see page 10)
I pound small broccoli florets
2 ounces canned anchovy fillets, drained
⅔ cup extra virgin olive oil
Ground black pepper
Cornmeal for dusting
2 cloves garlic, crushed
½ cup grated Parmesan cheese
2 tablespoons pine nuts

Prepare the dough. While waiting for the dough to rise, cook the broccoli florets in boiling, salted water for 3 minutes. Drain, and reserve a quarter of the florets.

Reserve four anchovy fillets, and chop the rest finely. Heat 5 tablespoons of the olive oil in a saucepan, and cook the chopped anchovies over a medium heat for 4-5 minutes, mashing them with the back of a spoon. Add the broccoli, and cook, stirring, for 2 minutes. Season and set aside.

When the dough is ready for use, divide it into two. Roll out the pizza dough as described on page 6. Make two 11-inch thin-crust bases. Place bases on baking sheets lightly dusted with cornmeal. Mix 4 tablespoons of the olive oil with the garlic, and brush on the pizzas. Divide the broccoli topping between the two pizzas, leaving a ½-inch border. Cut the reserved anchovies into slivers, and scatter them over the pizzas, with the Parmesan and the remaining olive oil.

Bake in a preheated oven at 475°F for 7 minutes. Remove, and scatter the reserved broccoli and the pine nuts over the pizzas. Return to the oven for 6-7 minutes, and serve immediately.

MAKES TWO 11-INCH PIZZAS

RIGHT: Pizza Frutti Di Mare

BLUE CHEESE, BACON & MUSHROOM PIZZA

Rich Pizza Dough (see page 10)
Cornmeal for dusting
2 tablespoons olive oil
¾ cup smooth cottage cheese
2 tablespoons milk
4 teaspoons snipped fresh chives
Salt and ground black pepper
6 ounces Dolcelatte cheese
4 slices cooked bacon
⅔ cup brown mushrooms

Prepare the dough. When it is ready for use, divide it into two equal portions. Roll out or stretch the pizza dough as described on page 6. Make two 11-inch thin-crust pizza bases. Place the bases on baking sheets lightly dusted with cornmeal, prick the center of each base several times with the prongs of a fork, and brush them all over with 1 tablespoon of the olive oil.

Mix the cottage cheese with the milk, chives and seasoning. Spread the mixture over the bases, leaving a ½-inch border. Slice the Dolcelatte cheese thinly, and arrange it in a spoke-like pattern over each pizza. Cut the bacon into 1-inch pieces, and scatter these evenly over the pizzas. Slice the mushrooms, and divide these between the pizzas. Grind over some black pepper, and drizzle the pizzas with the remaining olive oil.

Bake the pizzas in a preheated oven at 475°F for 12-13 minutes, until the crusts are golden and the cheese has melted. Serve at once.

MAKES TWO 11-INCH PIZZAS

MIXED MUSHROOM PIZZA

Cornmeal Dough (see page 10)
Cornmeal for dusting
3 tablespoons olive oil
2 cloves garlic, crushed
2 tablespoons chopped fresh parsley
4 tablespoons ricotta cheese
1 tablespoon milk
Salt and ground black pepper
⅓ cup butter
4 cups sliced mixed mushrooms, such as field, button, chestnut and girolles
2 teaspoons lemon juice
2 tablespoons snipped fresh chives
3 tablespoons grated pecorino cheese

Prepare the dough. When it is ready for use, divide it into two. Roll the dough as described on page 6. Make two 10-inch thin-crust pizza bases. Place the bases on baking sheets lightly dusted with cornmeal. Mix together 2 tablespoons of the oil with the garlic and parsley, and brush the oil over the bases.

Mix together the ricotta cheese and milk, season, and spread over the bases, leaving a 2-inch border.

Melt the butter in a large skillet, and add the remaining oil and mushrooms. Sauté over a high heat for 2 minutes. Remove from heat, season well, and stir in the lemon juice and chives. Spoon the mushrooms over the bases, leaving a ½-inch border. Sprinkle on the pecorino.

Bake in a preheated oven at 475°F for 12-15 minutes, until the crusts are crisp and the mushrooms cooked. Serve immediately.

MAKES TWO 10-INCH PIZZAS

TOP: Blue Cheese, Bacon & Mushroom Pizza
BOTTOM: Mixed Mushroom Pizza

SMOKED CHICKEN & PARSLEY PESTO PIZZA

Basic Pizza Dough, using herby variation with
chopped basil (see page 10)
Cornmeal for dusting
4 tablespoons olive oil
½ cup Fresh Parsley Pesto (see page 16)
8 halves sun-dried tomatoes in oil
6 ounces skinned smoked chicken
2 tablespoons grated Parmesan cheese
Ground black pepper
2 teaspoons chopped fresh parsley

Prepare the dough. When it is ready for use, divide it into two equal portions. Roll out or stretch the pizza dough as described on page 6. Make two 10-inch thin-crust pizza bases. Place the bases on baking sheets lightly dusted with cornmeal. Brush the bases all over with 2 tablespoons of the olive oil. Spread the Parsley Pesto over the bases, leaving a ½-inch border around the edges.

Bake the pizzas in a preheated oven at 475°F for 7 minutes and, while the pizzas are cooking, cut the sun-dried tomatoes into thick strips and slice the smoked chicken. Remove the pizzas from the oven, and scatter the tomatoes and chicken over them. Sprinkle with Parmesan and black pepper. Drizzle on the remaining olive oil.

Return the pizzas to the oven, and bake for a further 7 minutes, until crisp and golden. Remove from the oven, scatter with the parsley, and serve immediately.

MAKES TWO 10-INCH PIZZAS

PESTO, TOMATO & GARLIC PIZZA

Cornmeal Pizza Dough (see page 10)
Cornmeal for dusting
5 tablespoons extra virgin olive oil
4 tablespoons Fresh Basil Pesto (see page 16)
4 plum tomatoes
2 large cloves garlic
Salt and ground black pepper
2 tablespoons torn fresh basil leaves

Prepare the cornmeal dough. When it is ready for use, divide it into four equal portions. Roll out or stretch the pizza dough as described on page 6. Make four 7-inch thin-crust pizza bases. Place the bases on baking sheets lightly dusted with cornmeal, and brush them all over with 2 tablespoons of the olive oil. Mix another 2 tablespoons of oil with the pesto sauce, and spread this mixture over the four bases, leaving a ½-inch border.

Slice the tomatoes thickly. Peel the garlic, and slice the cloves into slivers. Divide the tomatoes and garlic between the four bases. Season with salt and pepper, and drizzle the remaining olive oil over the pizzas.

Bake the pizzas, in batches, in a preheated oven at 475°F for 10-12 minutes, until the crusts are crisp and golden. Remove from the oven, scatter with the basil leaves, and serve at once.

MAKES FOUR 7-INCH PIZZAS

RIGHT: Smoked Chicken & Parsley Pesto Pizza

SPRING VEGETABLE PIZZA

Cornmeal Pizza Dough (see page 10)
Cornmeal for dusting
3 tablespoons olive oil
2 cloves garlic, crushed
10 ounces mozzarella cheese
3 ounces pecorino cheese
12 stalks asparagus
2 small zucchini
10 yellow cherry tomatoes
4 scallions
2 tablespoons pine nuts
Salt and ground black pepper

Prepare the dough. When dough is ready for use, divide it into two equal portions. Roll out or stretch the pizza dough as described on page 6. Make two 10-inch thin-crust pizza bases. Place the bases on baking sheets lightly dusted with cornmeal. Mix together 2 tablespoons of the olive oil and the crushed garlic, and brush the oil over the pizza bases.

Slice the mozzarella cheese thinly, and grate the pecorino cheese. Divide the two cheeses between the bases, leaving a ½-inch border around the edges. Trim and cut the asparagus into 2-inch lengths, blanch briefly, and drain. Slice the zucchini, halve the cherry tomatoes, and cut the scallions into thick slices. Divide between the pizzas. Sprinkle on the pine nuts, season well, and drizzle on the remaining olive oil.

Bake the pizzas in a preheated oven at 475°F for 12-14 minutes, until crisp and golden. Serve at once.

MAKES TWO 10-INCH PIZZAS

PIZZA NICOISE

Whole-wheat Pizza Dough (see page 10)
Cornmeal for dusting
3 tablespoons extra virgin olive oil
1 cup Fresh Tomato & Herb Sauce (see page 12)
7 ounces canned tuna in oil
½ onion, very thinly sliced
12 black olives
Salt and ground black pepper
4 ounces thin green beans
2 tablespoons chopped fresh parsley

Prepare the dough. When it is ready for use, divide it into two equal portions. Roll or stretch the dough as described on page 6. Make two 11-inch thin-crust pizza bases. Place the bases on baking sheets dusted with cornmeal, and brush with half the olive oil.

Spread the Tomato & Herb Sauce over the bases, leaving a ½-inch border. Drain and flake the tuna. Divide it between the pizzas, with the onion slices and black olives. Season well, and drizzle on the remaining olive oil.

Bake the pizzas in a preheated oven at 475°F for 12 minutes. While they are cooking, top and tail the beans, and cut them into 1-inch lengths. Cook the beans in boiling, salted water for 4 minutes, then drain.

Remove the pizzas, scatter on the beans, and return to the oven for a further 3-4 minutes, until the crusts are crisp and golden. Remove from the oven, sprinkle with parsley, and serve.

MAKES TWO 11-INCH PIZZAS

LEFT: Spring Vegetable Pizza
RIGHT: Pizza Niçoise

PIZZA QUATTRO STAGIONI

Basic Pizza Dough (see page 10)
Cornmeal for dusting
3 tablespoons olive oil
¾ cup Basic Tomato Sauce (see page 12)

QUARTER I
2 tablespoons grated Parmesan cheese
2 large slices mortadella
2 marinated artichokes in oil, halved

QUARTER II
¼ cup butter
1 tablespoon oil
2 cloves garlic, finely chopped
1⅓ cups sliced, mixed mushrooms
Salt and ground black pepper

QUARTER III
1 cup chopped mozzarella cheese
2 small plum tomatoes, chopped
Salt and ground black pepper
8 large basil leaves, torn

QUARTER IV
¾ cup shelled, cooked mussels
½ teaspoon grated lemon zest
1 tablespoon olive oil
1 tablespoon chopped fresh oregano

Prepare the dough. When it is ready for use, divide it into two equal portions. Roll out or stretch the pizza dough as described on page 6. Make two 10-inch thin-crust pizza bases. Place the bases on baking sheets lightly dusted with cornmeal, and brush with 2 table-spoons of the olive oil. Spread the Basic Tomato Sauce over the pizza bases, leaving a ½-inch border around the edges.

Mark the four quarters on each pizza. For Quarter I on each pizza, sprinkle the Parmesan over the tomato sauce, slice the mortadella and place this over the cheese, and top with two halves of artichoke.

For Quarter II, heat the butter and oil in a saucepan and sauté the garlic and mushrooms for a couple of minutes. Season well, and divide this mixture between the second quarters on each pizza.

For Quarter III, mix together the ingredients and divide them between the third quarters on each pizza.

For Quarter IV, combine the ingredients, and divide them between the remaining quarters. Grind some black pepper over the two completed pizzas, and drizzle with the remaining olive oil.

Bake the pizzas in a preheated oven at 475°F for 12-15 minutes, until the crusts are crisp and golden and the topping cooked. Serve immediately.

MAKES TWO 10-INCH PIZZAS

RIGHT: Pizza Quattro Stagioni

PISSALADIERE PIZZA

Basic Pizza Dough (see page 10)
6 tablespoons olive oil
3 large red onions, very thinly sliced
Salt and ground black pepper
2 teaspoons superfine sugar
1 tablespoon chopped fresh oregano
Cornmeal for dusting
2 cloves garlic, crushed
½ cup Fresh Tomato & Herb Sauce (see page 12)
10 anchovy fillets
16 black olives

Prepare the dough. Prepare the onion topping while dough is rising. Heat 3 tablespoons of the oil in a heavy-bottomed pan, and cook the onions over a very low heat for 15-20 minutes, until they are soft but not browned. Season, and stir in the sugar and oregano. Set aside to cool.

Roll out or stretch pizza dough as described on page 6. Make two 10-inch thin-crust pizza bases. Place bases on baking sheets lightly dusted with cornmeal. Mix together 2 tablespoons of the olive oil and the crushed garlic, and brush this over the bases.

Divide the tomato sauce between the bases, leaving a ½-inch border around the edges. Divide the onions between the pizzas. Rinse the anchovy fillets, and dry them on paper towels. Slice them in half lengthwise. Use the anchovies to make a lattice pattern over the onion mixture. Stud with the black olives and drizzle the remaining oil over the pizzas.

Bake the pizzas in a preheated oven at 475°F for 12-14 minutes, until crisp and golden. Serve at once.

MAKES TWO 10-INCH PIZZAS

PUTTANESCA PIZZA

Cornmeal Pizza Dough or Whole-wheat Pizza Dough (see page 10)
Cornmeal for dusting
3 tablespoons olive oil
1 cup Tomato & Chili Sauce (see page 14)
2 plum tomatoes
1 large red chili
12 black olives
1 tablespoon capers
6 anchovies
2 tablespoons chopped fresh parsley
Ground black pepper

Prepare the dough. When it is ready for use, divide it into two. Roll or stretch the pizza dough as described on page 6. Make two 11-inch thin-crust pizza bases. Place bases on baking sheets dusted with cornmeal, and brush with half the olive oil.

Spread the Tomato & Chili Sauce over the bases, leaving a ½-inch border around the edges. Slice the tomatoes thickly, and add them to the pizzas. Slice the chili, and scatter the slices over the pizzas, along with the olives and capers. Rinse the anchovies, and dry them on paper towels; cut each in half lengthwise. Place three crosses of anchovy on each pizza. Drizzle on the remaining olive oil.

Bake the pizzas in a preheated oven at 475°F for 14-15 minutes, until the crusts are crisp and golden. Remove from the oven, and sprinkle with parsley and ground black pepper. Serve immediately.

MAKES TWO 11-INCH PIZZAS

TOP: Pissaladière Pizza
BOTTOM: Puttanesca Pizza

PIZZA SALUMERIA

Rich Pizza Dough (see page 10)
Cornmeal for dusting
3 tablespoons olive oil
2 teaspoons chopped fresh thyme
1 cup grated hard mozzarella cheese
¼ cup grated Parmesan cheese
8 slices Milano salami
8 slices hot Italian salami
4 slices prosciutto
4 slices bresaola
Ground black pepper
A few small thyme sprigs, to garnish

Prepare the dough. When it is ready for use, divide it into two. Cut off a small piece of dough from each portion, and set aside. Roll out the dough as described on page 6. Make two 9-inch thin-crust pizza bases. Place on baking sheets lightly dusted with cornmeal, and prick each base several times with a fork. Mix together 2 tablespoons of the oil and the 2 teaspoons of thyme, and brush this over the bases.

Cut each piece of reserved dough into two, and, with floured hands, shape each piece into a 'dough rope' that is long enough to stretch across the diameter of the pizza. Place two ropes at right angles across each pizza.

Mix together the two cheeses. Top all the pizza quarters with the cheese mixture, taking care to keep the dough ropes exposed. Spread cheese to ½ inch of the edges. Divide the cured meats between the quarters, drizzle on the remaining olive oil, and add black pepper.

Bake the pizzas in a preheated oven at 475°F for 12 minutes, until the crusts are golden. Remove, garnish with the thyme sprigs, and serve at once.

MAKES TWO 9-INCH PIZZAS

SICILIAN HOT PIZZA

Rich Pizza Dough (see page 10)
Cornmeal for dusting
3 tablespoons olive oil
¾ cup Tomato & Chili Sauce (see page 14)
8 large slices hot Italian salami
1 green bell pepper
1 green chili
½ onion
10 black olives
Ground black pepper

Prepare the dough. When it is ready for use, divide it into two equal portions. Roll out or stretch the pizza dough as described on page 6. Make two 10-inch thin-crust pizza bases. Place the bases on baking sheets lightly dusted with cornmeal, prick the center of each base several times with the prongs of a fork, and brush them all over with 2 tablespoons of the olive oil.

Spread the Tomato & Chili Sauce over the bases, leaving a ½-inch border. Arrange four slices of salami on each pizza. Slice the bell pepper into ten thin slices, remove the core and seeds, and divide the slices between the pizzas. Slice the chili and onion, and scatter on the pizza bases. Top each pizza with five olives, and drizzle on the remaining olive oil. Grind pepper over the top.

Bake the pizzas in a preheated oven at 475°F for 13-15 minutes, until crusts are crisp and golden. Remove from the oven, and serve at once.

MAKES TWO 10-INCH PIZZAS

RIGHT: Pizza Salumeria

DEEP-PAN PIZZAS

Deep-pan pizzas have thick bases and sides that form a shallow casing. They hold more topping than thin-crust pizzas, which makes them robust and satisfying. Deep-pan pizzas are either served whole as a main meal for those with good appetites, or cut into wedges or slices. Spicy Chorizo & Chickpea Pizza and Chinese Chicken Pizza are made as square pizzas, but can be cooked in the traditional round shape if preferred. Pizza Pasticcio uses pasta in a pizza case to create an unusual combination, while Chicago-style Stuffed Pizza Pie is based on the classic stuffed pizza developed by Italian immigrants to Chicago, and combines salami, broccoli and two cheeses in a cornmeal crust.

CHICAGO-STYLE STUFFED PIZZA PIE

Cornmeal Pizza Dough (see page 10),
made with 1 tablespoon rapid-rise
yeast, as suggested on page 6
Olive oil for brushing
Fresh Tomato & Herb Sauce (see page 12), to serve

STUFFING
6 ounces small broccoli florets
4 ounces salami, diced into small cubes
1 cup diced fontina cheese
1/3 cup grated Parmesan cheese
Salt and ground black pepper
6 tablespoons Fresh Tomato & Herb Sauce
(see page 12)

Prepare the dough. When it is ready for use, divide it into one-third and two-third portions. Roll and pull the two-thirds portion of dough to form a 13-inch circle. Oil an 11-inch deep-pan pizza pan, and press the prepared dough circle into the pan. Trim the top edge of the dough evenly. Prick the base of the dough several times with the prongs of a fork.

Prepare the stuffing. Blanch the broccoli in boiling, salted water for 3 minutes. Drain and refresh it, and place in a bowl. Add the salami, fontina cheese, 1/4 cup of the Parmesan, and season the mixture. Mix gently. Spread the tomato sauce over the pizza base. Top with the broccoli and cheese filling, and press down gently to produce an even layer.

Roll out the one-third portion of dough to make an 11-inch circle. Place this dough circle over the stuffed pizza, and press down gently onto the filling. Seal the two edges of dough together, and crimp the edges. Cut a small cross on top of the pizza lid to let steam escape. Brush the lid of the pizza with some olive oil.

Bake the pizza pie in the bottom of a preheated oven at 475°F for 10 minutes. Remove the pie from the oven, and sprinkle the remaining Parmesan cheese over the top. Return the pie to the top part of the oven, and bake for a further 20 minutes, until the crust is golden. Serve the pizza pie, cut into thick slices, with extra sauce.

MAKES ONE 11-INCH PIZZA PIE

RIGHT: Chicago-style Stuffed Pizza Pie

AMERICAN HOT PIZZA

2 purchased 9-inch deep-pan pizza bases
3 tablespoons olive oil
Cornmeal for dusting
¾ cup Roasted Pepper Sauce (see page 14)
¾ cup grated hard mozzarella cheese
2 x 4 ounce raw Italian sausages, skins removed
and crumbled
10 thick slices hot pepperoni salami
½ green bell pepper, cut into rings
½ yellow bell pepper, cut into rings
½ red onion, sliced
1-2 teaspoons dried chili flakes
1 fresh green chili, seeded and finely sliced
2 tablespoons grated pecorino cheese

Brush the two pizza bases all over with half the oil, and place them on baking sheets lightly dusted with cornmeal. Spread the pepper sauce over the two bases, leaving a ½-inch border around the edges. Scatter the mozzarella cheese over the sauce, along with the crumbled Italian sausage. Arrange the slices of pepperoni, pepper rings, and onion slices over the bases. Sprinkle on the dried chili flakes, and top with the fresh green chili and grated pecorino cheese. Drizzle the remaining olive oil over the pizzas.

Bake in a preheated oven at 425°F for 15-18 minutes, until the bases are crisp and the topping cooked. Remove the pizzas from the oven, and serve immediately.   MAKES TWO 9-INCH PIZZAS

PIZZA PARMA

Basic Pizza Dough (see page 10)
4 tablespoons olive oil
2 cloves garlic, crushed
Generous 1 cup Basic Tomato Sauce (see page 12)
8 ounces mozzarella cheese
8 thin slices prosciutto
10 small black olives
Ground black pepper

Prepare the dough. When it is ready for use, divide it into two equal portions, and shape it to fit two 9-inch oiled deep-dish pizza pans as described on page 8. Cover the pans with plastic wrap, and let the dough rise in a warm place for 30 minutes. Prick the dough with a fork at ½-inch intervals, and bake in a preheated oven at 475°F for 10 minutes.

Remove the bases from the oven. Mix together 3 tablespoons of the olive oil and the crushed garlic, and brush this mixture lightly over the pizza crusts. Spread the tomato sauce over the bases. Slice the mozzarella cheese into eight thick slices and arrange these on top of the pizzas, along with the slices of prosciutto. Scatter the black olives over, and top each pizza with freshly ground black pepper. Drizzle on the remaining olive oil.

Return the pizzas to the oven for a further 15 minutes, or until the crusts are golden and the topping cooked. Remove from the oven, and serve at once.
        MAKES TWO 9-INCH PIZZAS

TOP: Pizza Parma
BOTTOM: American Hot Pizza

PIZZA FLORENTINE

Basic Pizza Dough or Whole-wheat Pizza Dough
(see page 10)
3 tablespoons olive oil
12 ounces young leaf spinach
1 cup cream cheese
A little grated nutmeg
Salt and ground black pepper
4 small shallots, chopped
3 cloves garlic, crushed
2 large plum tomatoes, sliced
2 eggs

Prepare the dough. When it is ready for use, divide it into two equal portions, and shape it to fit two 9-inch oiled deep-dish pizza pans as described on page 8. Cover the pans with plastic wrap and let the dough rise in a warm place for 30 minutes. Prick the bases of the dough with a fork, and bake in a preheated oven at 475°F for 5 minutes.

Remove, and brush the crusts with 1 tablespoon of the olive oil. Steam the spinach lightly and reserve one-third. Process the rest of the spinach in a food processor with the cream cheese, nutmeg and seasoning. Transfer to a bowl.

Heat 2 tablespoons of the oil in a saucepan, and sauté the shallots and garlic for 5 minutes until soft; stir into the spinach mixture. Divide the mixture between the bases, and arrange the reserved spinach on the top. Arrange the tomato around the edge of each pizza.

Return to the oven for a further 16 minutes, then remove and crack an egg onto the center of each pizza. Return to the oven for a further 7-8 minutes, until the eggs are just set. Remove, and serve immediately. MAKES TWO 9-INCH PIZZAS

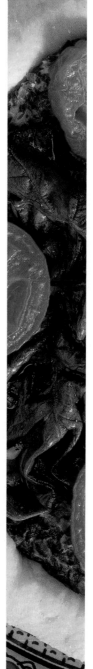

PIZZA NAPOLETANA

2 purchased 9-inch deep-pan pizza bases
2 tablespoons olive oil
Cornmeal for dusting
¾ cup Basic Tomato Sauce (see page 12)
2 small zucchini
1 small red onion
8 anchovies
4 teaspoons capers
10 kalamata olives
1 tablespoon fresh thyme leaves
Ground black pepper

Brush the pizza bases all over with half the olive oil. Place the bases on baking sheets lightly dusted with cornmeal, and spread them with the tomato sauce, leaving a ½-inch border around the edges.

Slice the zucchini thinly, and peel and slice the onion. Divide the zucchini and onion between the pizzas. Rinse the anchovy fillets, and dry them on paper towels. Halve the anchovies lengthwise, quarter them, and scatter them over the pizza bases, along with the capers, olives and thyme. Top each pizza with ground black pepper, and drizzle on the remaining olive oil.

Bake the pizzas in a preheated oven at 425°F for 16-18 minutes, until the bases are crisp and the topping cooked. Remove, and serve immediately.

MAKES TWO 9-INCH PIZZAS

RIGHT: Pizza Florentine

CHINESE CHICKEN PIZZA

Basic Pizza Dough (see page 10)
4 tablespoons peanut oil
1 teaspoon sesame oil
12 ounces skinless, boneless chicken,
cut into chunks
2 cloves garlic, finely chopped
6 tablespoons hoisin sauce
2 small red chilies, seeded and sliced
4 teaspoons sesame seeds
2 teaspoons soy sauce
6 scallions
1 small red bell pepper, seeded and cored, and cut
into small diamond shapes

Prepare the dough. When it is ready for use, divide it into two and shape to fit two 9-inch oiled square deep-dish pizza pans as described on page 8. Cover with plastic wrap and let rise for 30 minutes. Prick the bases with a fork, and bake in a preheated oven at 475°F for 5 minutes.

Remove from the oven. Mix together 2 tablespoons of the peanut oil and the sesame oil, and brush the pizza crusts lightly. Heat the remaining peanut oil in a pan, add the chicken and garlic, and cook over a high heat for 1-2 minutes. Remove, and stir in the hoisin sauce, red chilies, 2 tablespoons of the sesame seeds and the soy sauce. Slice the scallions thinly on the diagonal, reserve 3 tablespoons of the green tops, and stir the rest into the chicken mixture. Spoon the mixture over the pizza bases. Scatter the pepper diamonds and sesame seeds over the pizzas.

Return the pizzas to the oven for a further 16-18 minutes. Remove, sprinkle with the reserved scallion tops, and serve at once.

MAKES TWO 9-INCH PIZZAS

CHORIZO & CHICKPEA PIZZA

Basic Pizza Dough (see page 10)
5 tablespoons olive oil
1 onion, sliced
1 teaspoon ground cumin
1¼ cup cooked chickpeas
¾ cup Tomato & Chili Sauce (see page 14)
½ cup grated Gouda cheese
½ cup grated provolone cheese
20-24 thick slices chorizo sausage
6 rings each red and green bell peppers
2 pickled jalapeño chilies, sliced

Prepare the dough. When it is ready, divide it into two, and shape it to fit two 9-inch oiled square deep-dish pizza pans as described on page 8. Cover with plastic wrap and let rise for 30 minutes. Prick the bases with a fork, and bake in a preheated oven at 475°F for 5 minutes.

Remove and lightly brush 2 tablespoons of the olive oil over the crusts. Heat 2 tablespoons of the oil in a pan, and sauté the onion for 2 minutes; stir in the cumin and chickpeas, and cook for a further 2 minutes. Stir into the Tomato & Chili Sauce. Divide the sauce between the bases. Mix together the two cheeses, and sprinkle over the pizzas, along with the sliced chorizo. Drizzle on the remaining olive oil.

Return to the oven for a further 10 minutes. Remove, and divide the pepper and chilies between them. Bake for a further 10 minutes. Serve at once.

MAKES TWO 9-INCH PIZZAS

LEFT: Chinese Chicken Pizza
RIGHT: Chorizo & Chickpea Pizza

PIZZA PASTICCIO

Cornmeal Pizza Dough (see page 10)
6 tablespoons olive oil
Generous 1 cup Fresh Tomato & Herb Sauce
(see page 12)
1 pound young leaf spinach, steamed and squeezed
dry of excess moisture
1 large onion, chopped
2 cloves garlic, crushed
Salt and ground black pepper
2 tablespoons chopped fresh parsley
2 ounces spaghetti, cooked "al dente"
⅔ cup sour cream
½ cup grated hard mozzarella cheese
4 ounces smoked chicken, in thin strips
2 tablespoons grated Parmesan cheese

Prepare the dough. When it is ready for use, divide into two equal portions, and shape to fit two 9-inch oiled deep-dish pizza pans as described on page 8. Cover with plastic wrap, and let rise for 30 minutes. Prick the bases with a fork, and bake in a preheated oven at 475°F for 5 minutes.

Remove, and brush with 1 tablespoon of the olive oil. Spread the sauce over the bases, then a layer of spinach. (Use half the spinach.)

Heat 3 tablespoons of the oil in a pan, and cook the onion and garlic for 3 minutes; season well, and stir in the parsley, spaghetti, sour cream and mozzarella. Fold in the reserved spinach. Spoon the mixture over the bases and drizzle on the remaining olive oil.

Return the pizzas to the oven, and cook for 15 minutes. Remove, and scatter the chicken and Parmesan over the top, pressing down lightly. Bake for a further 5 minutes, and serve immediately.

MAKES TWO 9-INCH PIZZAS

HAM, PINEAPPLE & CORN PIZZA

Basic Pizza Dough (see page 10)
Olive oil for brushing
1 cup Corn Sauce (see page 16)
1 cup grated mozzarella cheese
⅓ cup grated Parmesan cheese
4 tablespoons snipped fresh chives
Salt and ground black pepper
6 slices honey-roast ham
4 slices fresh pineapple, cores removed

Prepare the dough. When it is ready for use, divide it into two equal portions, and roll and shape it to fit two 9-inch oiled deep-dish pizza pans as described on page 8. Cover the pans with plastic wrap and let the dough rise in a warm place for 30 minutes. Prick the bases of the dough with a fork, and bake in a preheated oven at 475°F for 5 minutes.

Remove the bases from the oven, and brush the crusts lightly with olive oil. Spread the Corn Sauce over the bases. Mix the mozzarella with most of the Parmesan (reserving 2 tablespoons of Parmesan for sprinkling) and the snipped chives. Season the mixture well, and spoon it over the Corn Sauce. Cut the ham into thick strips and the pineapple slices into chunks; divide between the pizzas. Top with black pepper and the reserved Parmesan. Drizzle a little olive oil over the pizzas.

Return the pizzas to the oven for 15-20 minutes, until the crusts are golden and the topping cooked. Remove, and serve at once.

MAKES TWO 9-INCH PIZZAS

RIGHT: Pizza Pasticcio

PIZZA PESCATORE

Rich Pizza Dough (see page 10)
3 tablespoons olive oil
2 tablespoons chopped fresh parsley
1½ cups Corn Sauce (see page 16)
6 ounces mixed seafood preserved in oil, such as
mussels, octopus and baby squid
5 ounces fresh or canned salmon
¾ cup grated Parmesan cheese
Ground black pepper
2 tablespoons snipped fresh chervil

Prepare the dough. When it is ready for use, divide it
into two equal portions, and roll and shape it to fit two
9-inch oiled deep-dish pizza pans as described on page
8. Cover the pans with plastic wrap and let the dough
rise in a warm place for 30 minutes. Prick the bases of
the dough with a fork at ½-inch intervals, and bake in a
preheated oven at 475°F for 10 minutes.

Remove the bases from the oven. Mix together the
olive oil and parsley, and brush this mixture lightly
over the pizza crusts. Spread the Corn Sauce over the
bases. Divide the mixed seafood between the two pizzas. Break the salmon into large flakes, and divide between the pizzas. Sprinkle the Parmesan and ground
black pepper over the top.

Return the pizzas to the oven, and bake for a further
12-15 minutes, until the seafood and sauce are warmed
through and the salmon is cooked. Remove from the
oven, sprinkle with the chervil, and serve at once.

MAKES TWO 9-INCH PIZZAS

GREEK-STYLE PIZZA

Basic Pizza Dough (see page 10)
4 tablespoons olive oil
1 small onion, chopped
2 cloves garlic, crushed
2 cups ground lamb
2 tablespoons tomato paste
4 teaspoons chopped fresh parsley
Salt and ground black pepper
½ cup Basic Tomato Sauce (see page 12)
12 thin slices eggplant
1 cup crumbled feta cheese
2 teaspoons chopped fresh oregano

Prepare the dough. When it is ready, divide into two
and shape to fit two 9-inch oiled deep-dish pizza pans
as described on page 8. Cover the pans with plastic
wrap and let rise in a warm place for 30 minutes.

Heat 1 tablespoon of the oil in a pan, and sauté the
onion and garlic for 3-4 minutes. Add the lamb and
cook for 5 minutes. Stir in the tomato paste, parsley
and seasoning, and cook for a further 10 minutes.

Prick the bases of the dough with a fork, and bake in
a preheated oven at 475°F for 5 minutes. Remove, and
brush the crusts with 1 tablespoon of the olive oil.
Spread the sauce over the bases, and divide the filling
between the pizzas. Brush the eggplant with the remaining olive oil, and season. Scatter the feta cheese
and egg plant over the pizzas.

Return the pizzas to the oven for 15-20 minutes,
until the crusts and feta are golden. Remove, sprinkle
with oregano, and serve at once.

MAKES TWO 9-INCH PIZZAS

TOP: Pizza Pescatore
BOTTOM: Greek-style Pizza

CHILI CON CARNE PIZZA

Cornmeal Pizza Dough (see page 10)
4 tablespoons olive oil
1 onion, chopped
2 cloves garlic, crushed
1 teaspoon ground cumin
1 teaspoon chili powder
2 cups ground beef
1¾ cups canned chopped tomatoes
1 teaspoon dried oregano
1 tablespoon molasses
1 tablespoon tomato paste
2 cups canned red kidney beans, drained
Salt and ground black pepper
¾ cup grated Cheddar cheese
4 tablespoons sour cream
4 teaspoons chopped fresh cilantro

Prepare the dough. When it is ready for use, divide it into two, and shape to fit two 9-inch oiled deep-dish pizza pans as described on page 8. Cover the pans with plastic wrap and leave to rise in a warm place for 30 minutes.

Heat 2 tablespoons of the oil in a pan, and sauté the onion and garlic for 2 minutes. Stir in the cumin and chili powder, and cook for a further minute. Add the beef and cook, stirring, for 3-4 minutes. Stir in the tomatoes and oregano, and simmer for 30 minutes. Add the molasses, tomato paste, kidney beans and seasoning, and cook for 15 minutes.

Prick the bases with a fork, and bake in a preheated oven at 475°F for 10 minutes. Remove, and brush with the remaining oil. Divide the chili con carne between the pizzas, and sprinkle the cheese over the top.

Return to the oven for 15-20 minutes. Remove, and drizzle each pizza with sour cream. Sprinkle on the cilantro, and serve at once.

MAKES TWO 9-INCH PIZZAS

ENGLISH CHEESE PIZZA

Basic Pizza Dough (see page 10)
Olive oil for brushing
6 tablespoons Basic Tomato Sauce (see page 12)
1 cup grated red Leicester cheese
2 tablespoons chopped walnut pieces
⅓ cup cream cheese
Salt and ground black pepper
1 cup crumbled Stilton cheese
1 cup grated Cheddar cheese
2 tablespoons snipped fresh chives

Prepare the dough. When it is ready for use, divide it into two, and roll and shape it to fit two 9-inch oiled deep-dish pizza pans as described on page 8. Cover the pans with plastic wrap, and leave in a warm place for 30 minutes. Prick the bases with a fork, and bake in a preheated oven at 475°F for 10 minutes.

Remove the bases from the oven, and brush lightly with olive oil. Spread the tomato sauce over the bases. Mix together the red Leicester cheese and walnuts, and divide over a third of each pizza base. Mix the cream cheese with some salt and pepper, and spoon it over the second third of each pizza base. Scatter the crumbled Stilton cheese over the cream cheese. Mix together the Cheddar and chives, and divide the mixture over the last third of each pizza base. Top with black pepper.

Return the pizzas to the oven for a further 15 minutes, or until the cheese topping has melted. Remove, and serve at once.

MAKES TWO 9-INCH PIZZAS

RIGHT: Chili Con Carne Pizza

CALZONES & SFINCIONES

This chapter includes two often-neglected types of pizza which deserve greater recognition. A calzone is a folded pizza, encasing a filling. Calzones can be either deep-fried or oven-baked, producing different textures in the cooked dough. A sfincione is a stuffed flat pie originally from Sicily. It should be served cut into thick wedges.

CHICKEN & CORN CALZONE

Basic Pizza Dough (see page 10)
1 egg white, lightly beaten
Oil for deep-frying

FILLING
4 slices bacon
2 cups skinned and diced smoked chicken
1 cup Corn Sauce (see page 16)
1 scallion, chopped
Salt and ground black pepper

Prepare the dough. While the dough is proving, make the filling.

Broil the bacon slices for 3 minutes on each side until crisp. Let cool, then snip into bite-sized pieces. Place in a bowl with the rest of the filling ingredients, and mix well.

When the dough is ready for use, divide it into five equal portions. Roll out each portion to produce a 7-inch circle. Place one-fifth of the filling on one half of each dough circle. Brush the edges of each circle with a little egg white, and fold the circle over. Seal the edges, crimping them if desired.

Heat the oil for deep-frying and fry the calzones for 5 minutes until golden. Remove with a slotted spoon, and drain on paper towels. Serve at once.

MAKES FIVE 7-INCH CALZONES

CALZONE CAPONATA

Basic Pizza Dough (see page 10)
Olive oil for brushing
Roasted Pepper Sauce (see page 14), to serve

FILLING
2 tablespoons olive oil
1 medium onion, chopped
2 cloves garlic, crushed
½ cup diced eggplant
½ cup diced zucchini
½ red bell pepper, diced
½ green bell pepper, diced
1 stalk celery, chopped
4 anchovies, chopped
1 tablespoon capers
2 tablespoons chopped fresh basil
1 cup diced mozzarella cheese
Salt and ground black pepper

Prepare the dough. While the dough is rising, heat the oil in a saucepan, and cook the onion and garlic for 2 minutes. Add the eggplant and zucchini, and cook for 4 minutes. Add the peppers, celery and anchovies for a further 2 minutes. Remove, and stir in the capers, basil, mozzarella and seasoning.

When the dough is ready, divide it into five. Roll out each portion to produce a 7-inch circle. Place one-fifth of the filling on one half of each circle. Brush the edges with a little water, and fold over. Seal the edges.

Place the calzones on baking sheets. Brush with olive oil. Bake in a preheated oven at 475°F for 15-20 minutes. Serve with Roasted Pepper Sauce.

MAKES FIVE 7-INCH CALZONES

TOP: Chicken & Corn Calzone
BOTTOM: Calzone Caponata

ZUCCHINI & SMOKED HAM CALZONE

Basic Pizza Dough (see page 10)
1 egg white, lightly beaten
Oil for deep-frying

FILLING

2 tablespoons olive oil
5 small shallots, peeled and chopped
2 cloves garlic, crushed
5 ounces zucchini
Salt and ground black pepper
5 ounces smoked ham
1¼ cups grated Cheddar cheese

Prepare the dough. While the dough is rising, make the filling.

Heat the oil in a saucepan. Add the shallots and garlic, and sauté for 4-5 minutes. Cut the zucchini into julienne strips, add them to the pan, and cook for a further 2 minutes. Season the mixture well, then transfer it to a bowl and leave to cool. Slice the ham into thin strips. Stir the ham and cheese into the cooled onion and zucchini mixture.

When the dough is ready for use, divide it into five equal portions. Roll out each portion to produce a 7-inch circle. Place one-fifth of the filling on one half of each dough circle. Brush the edges of each circle with a little beaten egg white, and fold the circles over to produce five semi-circles. Seal the edges of each calzone well.

Heat the oil for deep-frying. When it is hot enough, fry the calzones in batches for 5 minutes at a time, until crisp and golden. Remove from the oil with a slotted spoon, and drain on paper towels. Serve at once.

MAKES FIVE 7-INCH CALZONES

CALZONE CARBONARA

Basic Pizza Dough (see page 10)
Cornmeal for dusting
Olive oil for brushing
5 teaspoons freshly grated Parmesan cheese

FILLING

4 tablespoons olive oil
20 slices bacon, chopped
3 cloves garlic, crushed
1¾ cups cream cheese
1 egg yolk
Salt and ground black pepper

Prepare the dough. While the dough is rising, make the filling.

Heat the oil in a skillet. Add the bacon and garlic, and cook for 6 minutes until golden. Drain on paper towels, and let cool. Mix together the cream cheese and egg yolk, and season. Stir the bacon and garlic into the cream cheese mixture.

When the dough is ready for use, divide it into five equal portions. Roll out each portion to produce a 7-inch circle. Place one-fifth of the filling on one half of each dough circle. Brush the edges of each circle with a little water, and fold the circles over to produce five semi-circles. Seal the edges well.

Place the calzones on baking sheets lightly dusted with cornmeal. Brush with olive oil, and sprinkle with Parmesan cheese. Bake in a preheated oven at 475°F for 15 minutes, until crisp and golden. Remove from the oven, and serve at once.

MAKES FIVE 7-INCH CALZONES

RIGHT: Zucchini & Smoked Ham Calzone

AVOCADO, SCAMORZA & TOMATO CALZONE

Basic Pizza Dough (see page 10)
Cornmeal for dusting
Olive oil for brushing
5 teaspoons freshly grated Parmesan cheese

FILLING

5 ounces scamorza cheese (smoked mozzarella)
1 large avocado
2 small tomatoes
4 teaspoons snipped fresh chives
4 teaspoons chopped fresh parsley
Salt and ground black pepper

Prepare the dough. While the dough is rising, make the filling.

Dice the scamorza and place it in a bowl. Peel the avocado, and remove the stone; dice the flesh and add it to the cheese. Dice the tomato, and add it to the bowl, along with the herbs and seasoning. Mix the ingredients well to combine.

When the dough is ready for use, divide it into five equal portions. Roll out each portion to produce a 7-inch circle. Place one-fifth of the filling on one half of each dough circle. Brush the edges of each circle with a little water, and fold the circles over to produce five semi-circles. Seal the edges of each calzone well.

Place the calzones on baking sheets lightly dusted with cornmeal. Brush with olive oil, and sprinkle with Parmesan cheese. Bake in a preheated oven at 475°F for 15 minutes, until crisp and golden. Remove from the oven, and serve at once.

MAKES FIVE 7-INCH CALZONES

SPICY BEEF CALZONE

Basic Pizza Dough (see page 10)
1 egg white, lightly beaten
Oil for deep-frying

FILLING

3 tablespoons vegetable oil
2 small onions, peeled and chopped
3 cloves garlic, crushed
1 green chili, seeded and sliced
2½ cups lean ground beef
5 teaspoons tomato paste
1-1½ teaspoons paprika
1 large tomato, chopped
Salt and ground black pepper
1¼ cups diced fontana cheese

Prepare the dough. While the dough is rising, make the filling.

Heat the oil in a pan, and sauté the onion and garlic for 3 minutes. Add the chili, and cook for a further minute. Stir in the beef and cook, stirring constantly, for 4 minutes. Add the tomato paste, paprika, tomato and seasoning, and cook for a further 4 minutes. Leave to cool. Stir in the diced cheese.

When the dough is ready for use, divide it into five. Roll out each portion to produce a 7-inch circle. Place one-fifth of the filling on one half of each dough circle. Brush the edges of each circle with a little beaten egg white, and fold the circles over. Seal the edges.

Heat the oil for deep-frying and fry the calzones in batches for 5 minutes at a time, until golden. Remove from the oil with a slotted spoon, and drain on paper towels. Serve immediately.

MAKES FIVE 7-INCH CALZONES

TOP: Avocado, Scamorza & Tomato Calzone
BOTTOM: Spicy Beef Calzone

SPINACH & PINE NUT CALZONE

Cornmeal Pizza Dough (see page 10)
Cornmeal for dusting
Olive oil for brushing

FILLING
1¾ cups cooked spinach
1¼ cups ricotta cheese
5 tablespoons toasted pine nuts
5 tablespoons grated Parmesan cheese
5 teaspoons sun-dried tomato paste
Salt and ground black pepper

Prepare the dough. While the dough is rising, make the filling.

Squeeze any excess moisture from the spinach. Chop the spinach, and place it in a mixing bowl. Add the remaining ingredients, and mix well.

When the dough is ready for use, divide it into five equal portions. Roll out each portion to produce a 7-inch circle. Place one-fifth of the filling on one half of each dough circle. Brush the edges of each circle with a little water, and fold the circles over to produce five semi-circles. Seal the edges of each calzone well to enclose the filling.

Place the calzones on baking sheets lightly dusted with cornmeal. Brush with olive oil. Bake in a pre-heated oven at 475°F for 15 minutes, until crisp and golden. Remove from the oven, and serve at once.

MAKES FIVE 7-INCH CALZONES

THREE-CHEESE CALZONE

Basic Pizza Dough, using herby variation
(see page 10)
Cornmeal for dusting
Olive oil for brushing
Fresh Tomato & Herb Sauce (see page 12), to serve

FILLING
⅔ cup ricotta cheese
1¼ cups grated Emmental cheese
1¼ cups grated Parmesan cheese
5 halves sun-dried tomatoes in oil, chopped
10 black olives, pitted and chopped
5 teaspoons snipped fresh chives
Salt and ground black pepper

Prepare the dough. While the dough is rising, make the filling.

Place all the ingredients for the filling in a large bowl, and mix well. Set aside.

When the dough is ready for use, divide it into five equal portions. Roll out each portion to produce a 7-inch circle. Place one-fifth of the filling on one half of each dough circle. Brush the edges of each circle with a little water, and fold the circles over. Seal the edges.

Place the calzones on baking sheets lightly dusted with cornmeal. Brush with olive oil. Bake in a pre-heated oven at 475°F for 15 minutes, until golden. Remove, and serve with Fresh Tomato & Herb Sauce.

MAKES FIVE 7-INCH CALZONES

RIGHT: Spinach & Pine Nut Calzone

SEAFOOD CALZONE

Basic Pizza Dough (see page 10)
Cornmeal for dusting
Olive oil for brushing
4 teaspoons freshly grated pecorino cheese

FILLING
4 tablespoons olive oil
4 small shallots, chopped
¾ cup cooked, peeled shrimp
1½ cups chopped scallops
1 cup shelled, cooked mussels
½ teaspoon saffron strands, infused in
2 tablespoons water for 10 minutes
Salt and ground black pepper
1 cup diced mozzarella cheese
4 teaspoons chopped fresh chervil

Prepare the dough. While the dough is rising, make the filling.

Heat the oil in a large saucepan. Add the shallots, and cook for 3 minutes. Add the prepared seafood, and cook for 4 minutes. Stir in the saffron strands with the water, and season. Let cool slightly. Stir in the mozzarella and chervil.

When the dough is ready for use, divide it into four. Roll out each portion to produce a 9-inch circle. Place one-quarter of the filling on one half of each dough circle. Brush the edges of each circle with a little water, and fold the circles over. Seal the edges.

Place the calzones on baking sheets lightly dusted with cornmeal. Brush with olive oil and sprinkle with pecorino cheese. Bake in a preheated oven at 475°F for 15-20 minutes. Remove, and serve at once.

MAKES FOUR 9-INCH CALZONES

TOP: Salt Cod Calzone
BOTTOM: Seafood Calzone

SALT COD CALZONE

Basic Pizza Dough, using herby variation, cilantro as the herb (see page 10)
Olive oil for brushing
4 tablespoons grated provolone cheese
Basic Tomato Sauce (see page 12), to serve

FILLING
6 ounces salt cod
1 large clove garlic, crushed
5 tablespoons each milk and extra virgin olive oil
½ cup smooth cottage cheese
3 tablespoons chopped fresh cilantro
8 stuffed olives, sliced
1 tablespoon olive oil
¾ cup sliced leeks

Soak the salt cod in cold water for 24 hours, changing the water three or four times.

Prepare the dough. While the dough is rising, place the cod in a pan of fresh water. Bring it to a boil, then simmer for 8-10 minutes. Drain and let cool. Remove the skin and bones, and flake the flesh. Place the flaked fish in a food processor with the garlic. Process briefly. Combine the milk with the extra virgin olive oil, and pour into the processor with the motor running. Add the cottage cheese and cilantro and process briefly. Transfer to a bowl, and stir in the olives. Heat the olive oil in a pan, and sauté the leeks for 1 minute. Stir the leeks into the cod mixture.

When the dough is ready, divide it into four. Roll out each portion to produce a 9-inch circle. Place one-quarter of the filling on one half of each circle. Brush the edges with water, fold over, and seal.

Place the calzones on baking sheets. Brush with olive oil and sprinkle 1 tablespoon of provolone over each. Bake in a preheated oven at 475°F for 15-20 minutes. Remove, and serve with the sauce.

MAKES FOUR 9-INCH CALZONES

ITALIAN SAUSAGE & LEEK SFINCIONE

Basic Pizza Dough (see page 10)
Cornmeal for dusting
Olive oil for brushing
Basic Tomato Sauce (see page 12), to serve

FILLING

2 tablespoons olive oil
½ onion, sliced
2 small leeks, chopped
2 Italian sausages, sliced
Salt and ground black pepper
1 cup grated mozzarella cheese

Prepare the dough. While the dough is rising, prepare the filling.

Heat the oil in a pan, and sauté the onion for 4 minutes. Add the leeks for a further minute. Stir in the sliced sausages, and cook for 2 more minutes. Remove from the heat, season, and leave to cool. Stir in the diced mozzarella.

When the dough is ready for use, divide it into two equal portions. Roll out one portion to produce a 10-inch circle. Place the circle on a baking sheet lightly dusted with cornmeal, and spread the filling over the circle, leaving a 2-inch border. Roll out the remaining portion of dough to produce another 10-inch circle. Dampen the edges of the first circle with water, and place the remaining circle on top. Press down gently. Seal the edges, and cut a cross in the top.

Brush liberally with olive oil, and bake in a pre-heated oven at 475°F for 20-25 minutes. Serve hot, cut into thick wedges, passing the sauce separately.

MAKES ONE SFINCIONE

RIGHT: Italian Sausage & Leek Sfincione

VEGETABLE SFINCIONE

Cornmeal Pizza Dough (see page 10)
Cornmeal for dusting
Olive oil for brushing
1 tablespoon grated Parmesan cheese

FILLING

1 red bell pepper, quartered and cored
1 orange bell pepper, quartered and cored
1 large red onion, thickly sliced lengthways
3 tablespoons olive oil
5 ounces creamy, soft goat cheese
1 clove garlic, crushed
2 teaspoons chopped fresh thyme
Salt and ground black pepper

Prepare the dough. While the dough is rising, prepare the filling.

Place the bell peppers, skin-side up, on a rack, and broil for 12 minutes, until the skins are charred. When cool, peel off and discard their skins. Place the onion slices on a rack, and brush with half the olive oil. Broil for 3 minutes. Turn them over, brush with oil, and broil for 3 minutes. Let cool. Place the cheese, garlic, thyme and seasoning in a bowl, and mix well.

When the dough is ready, divide it into two. Roll out one portion to produce a 10-inch circle. Place the circle on a baking sheet lightly dusted with cornmeal. Place half the red onion and the orange pepper on the dough circle, leaving a 2-inch border. Top with the cheese mixture, and remaining onion and red pepper.

Roll out the remaining portion of dough to produce another 10-inch circle. Dampen the edges of the first circle, and place the remaining circle on top. Press down gently. Seal the edges and cut a cross in the top. Brush with olive oil, and sprinkle on the Parmesan.

Bake in a preheated oven at 475°F for 20-25 minutes. Serve hot, cut into thick wedges.

MAKES ONE SFINCIONE

FENNEL SFINCIONE

Basic Pizza Dough (see page 10)
Cornmeal for dusting
Walnut oil for brushing

FILLING
¾ cup sliced fennel
3 tablespoons olive oil
I small red bell pepper, sliced
½ onion, sliced
I clove garlic, crushed
½ cup cubed Bel Paese cheese
3 tablespoons smooth cottage cheese
I tablespoon chopped fresh parsley
¼ cup pistachio nuts
Salt and ground black pepper

Prepare the dough. While the dough is rising, prepare the filling.

Blanch the fennel for 1½ minutes; drain and refresh under cold water. Heat the oil in a large pan, and sauté the onion and garlic for 2 minutes. Add the fennel and red pepper, and sauté for a further 3 minutes. Transfer to a bowl and let cool. Add the two cheeses, parsley, pistachios and seasoning, and mix well.

When the dough is ready for use, divide it into two. Roll out one portion to produce a 10-inch circle. Place the circle on a baking sheet lightly dusted with cornmeal. Spread the filling over the circle, leaving a 2-inch border. Roll out the remaining portion of dough to produce another 10-inch circle. Dampen the edges of the first circle with water, and place the other circle on top. Press down gently, and seal the edges. Cut a cross in the top. Brush with olive oil.

Bake in a preheated oven at 475°F for 20-25 minutes. Serve hot, cut into thick wedges.

MAKES ONE SFINCIONE

GORGONZOLA, ARTICHOKE & SALAMI SFINCIONE

Cornmeal Pizza Dough (see page 10)
Cornmeal for dusting
2 tablespoons walnut oil
2 tablespoons chopped walnuts

FILLING
¾ cup cubed Gorgonzola cheese
2 ounces Milano salami, cut into thin strips
2 artichoke hearts marinated in oil, cut into bite-sized pieces
¼ cup ricotta cheese
I tablespoon snipped fresh chives
Ground black pepper

Prepare the dough. While the dough is rising, place all the ingredients for the filling in a large bowl, and mix gently. Set aside.

When the dough is ready for use, divide it into two equal portions. Roll out one portion to produce a 10-inch circle. Place the circle on a baking sheet lightly dusted with cornmeal. Spread the filling over the circle, leaving a 2-inch border around the edges. Roll out the remaining portion of dough to produce another 10-inch circle. Dampen the edges of the first circle with water, and place the remaining circle on top. Press down gently, and seal the edges. Cut a cross in the top. Brush with walnut oil, and scatter the chopped walnuts on top.

Bake in a preheated oven at 475°F for 20-25 minutes until golden. Serve hot, cut into thick wedges.

MAKES ONE SFINCIONE

TOP: Fennel Sfincione
BOTTOM: Gorgonzola, Artichoke & Salami Sfincione

SPECIALTY PIZZAS

This chapter creates pizzas in the broadest sense, using all sorts of bases, from French bread and focaccia to puff pastry and naan bread. These pizzas are small, and suitable for light snacks or party food. Some use very simple basic ingredients, while others are more exotic. Dessert pizzas have also been included. Banana, Rum & Raisin Pizza has a Caribbean flavor while Calzone Sorpresa will appeal to chocoholics.

PROSCIUTTO & FIG PIZZAS

4 purchased 6-inch thin-crust pizza bases
4 tablespoons extra virgin olive oil
2 cloves garlic, crushed
8 slices prosciutto
4 ripe fresh figs
Ground black pepper

Place the pizza bases on two baking sheets. Mix together 2 tablespoons of the olive oil and the crushed garlic. Brush all over the bases.

Bake the pizza bases in a preheated oven at 425°F for 10 minutes. Remove from the oven, and top each pizza with two slices of prosciutto. Peel the figs, if desired, and slice each fig into four. Arrange the sliced fig over the prosciutto, and top each pizza with a generous grinding of black pepper. Drizzle the remaining olive oil over the pizzas.

Return the pizzas to the oven, and bake for a further 3-4 minutes to warm the topping. Remove from the oven, and serve at once.

MAKES FOUR 6-INCH MINI PIZZAS

EGGPLANT PIZZAS

Basic Pizza Dough, using herby variation
(see page 10)
Cornmeal for dusting
Scant ½ cup olive oil
½ cup Basic Tomato Sauce (see page 12)
Salt and ground black pepper
1 cup crumbled feta cheese
1 medium eggplant
8 sun-dried tomatoes in oil, cut into strips

Prepare the dough as described in the basic recipe. When it is ready for use, divide it into eight equal portions. Roll out pizza dough as described on page 6. Make eight 4-inch thin-crust pizza bases. Place bases on baking sheets lightly dusted with cornmeal, and brush with 3 tablespoons of the olive oil.

Spread 1 tablespoon of the tomato sauce over each pizza, leaving a ½-inch border. Divide the feta cheese between the pizzas. Slice the eggplant into sixteen very thin slices, and brush with the remaining olive oil. Season well, and place two slices on each pizza. Top with ground black pepper.

Bake the pizzas in a preheated oven at 475°F for 8 minutes. Remove from the oven, and scatter evenly with the sun-dried tomato strips. Return the pizzas to the oven, and bake for a further 5 minutes. Remove from the oven, and serve immediately.

MAKES EIGHT 4-INCH MINI PIZZAS

TOP: Eggplant Pizzas
BOTTOM: Prosciutto & Fig Pizza

BRIE & CHERRY TOMATO MINI PIZZAS

Basic Pizza Dough (see page 10)
Cornmeal for dusting
6 tablespoons olive oil
1 cup Fresh Basil Pesto (see page 16)
1¼ pounds Brie, sliced thinly
20 cherry tomatoes, halved
Ground black pepper
5 large basil leaves, torn

Prepare the dough. When it is ready for use, divide it into ten equal portions. Roll out or stretch the pizza dough as described on page 6. Make ten 4-inch thin-crust pizza bases. Place the bases on baking sheets lightly dusted with cornmeal, and brush them all over with 3 tablespoons of the olive oil.

Spread the basil pesto evenly over the pizzas, leaving a ¼-inch border around the edges. Divide the slices of Brie between the pizzas. Place four halves of cherry tomato on each pizza, and top with some black pepper. Drizzle the remaining olive oil over the pizzas.

Bake the pizzas in a preheated oven at 475°F for 12-13 minutes, until crusts are golden and the cheese has melted. Remove from the oven, and sprinkle with basil. Serve at once.

MAKES TEN 4-INCH MINI PIZZAS

LAMB TIKKA MINI PIZZAS

1 tablespoon olive oil
½ onion, chopped
1 clove garlic, crushed
1½ cups cubed lamb neck fillet
2 tablespoons tikka paste
6 purchased mini garlic naan breads
¼ cup smooth cottage cheese
1 tablespoon natural yogurt
1 tablespoon chopped fresh mint

Prepare the lamb tikka. Heat the oil in a saucepan, and sauté the onion and garlic for 3 minutes until soft. Add the lamb, and cook for a further 3 minutes. Stir in the tikka paste, and cook over a medium heat for 10 minutes, until the lamb is tender.

Place the naan breads on baking sheets. Mix the cottage cheese with the yogurt, and spread over the naan breads, leaving a ½-inch border around the edges. Top each naan bread with some of the lamb tikka.

Bake the pizzas in a preheated oven at 350°F for 6-8 minutes, until they are warmed through. Remove, sprinkle with chopped mint, and serve at once.

MAKES SIX MINI PIZZAS

Variation: If you prefer, substitute diced, skinless, boneless chicken breast or diced monkfish for the lamb. If making fish tikka, cook the monkfish for only 5 minutes instead of the 10 minutes suggested for lamb. Chicken needs the same cooking time as lamb.

LEFT: Brie & Cherry Tomato Mini Pizzas
RIGHT: Lamb Tikka Mini Pizzas

CHECKERBOARD PIZZA

Basic Pizza Dough, using herby variation
(see page 10)
Cornmeal for dusting
3 tablespoons olive oil

ROASTED PEPPER TOPPING
2 red bell peppers
1 yellow bell pepper
4 tablespoons olive oil
Salt and ground black pepper
½ cup Fresh Tomato & Herb Sauce (see page 12)

GOAT CHEESE AND BLACK
OLIVE TOPPING
4 tablespoons black olive tapenade
9 thin slices goat cheese
1 tablespoon fresh rosemary leaves
1 tablespoon fresh thyme leaves
Ground black pepper
2 tablespoons olive oil

Prepare the dough as described in the basic recipe. When it is ready for use, divide it into two equal portions, and roll out until it is ¼-inch thick. Cut nine 3-inch squares from each portion of dough. Place the eighteen squares of dough on baking sheets lightly dusted with cornmeal. Brush the dough squares all over with the olive oil.

Prepare the roasted pepper topping. Halve the bell peppers and remove the cores. Place them, skin-side up, under a hot broiler and broil for 5-6 minutes, until the skins begin to blacken. Remove the peppers from the heat, and let them cool. Peel off the skins, and slice the pepper flesh into thin strips. Mix the sliced peppers with the olive oil, and season them well with salt and pepper.

Top nine of the dough squares with pepper topping: divide the Fresh Tomato & Herb Sauce between the squares and spread it over the bases, leaving a ¼-inch border around the edges. Top each base with some roasted pepper strips.

Top the remaining dough squares with goat cheese topping. Spread the tapenade over the bases, leaving a ¼-inch border around the edges, and top each base with a slice of goat cheese. Sprinkle with the fresh herbs, season with ground black pepper, and drizzle with the olive oil.

Bake the pizza squares in a preheated oven at 475°F for 12-13 minutes, until crusts are golden. Remove from the oven, and arrange alternate squares of roast pepper and goat cheese pizza on a board to produce a checkerboard effect.

MAKES EIGHTEEN MINI PIZZAS

RIGHT: Checkerboard Pizzas

FRENCH BREAD PIZZA MARGHERITA

2 pieces French bread, about 5 inches long
¼ cup butter
2 tablespoons chopped fresh basil
2 large beef tomatoes
½ cup diced mozzarella cheese
Salt and ground black pepper
I tablespoon grated Parmesan cheese
I tablespoon extra virgin olive oil
4 large basil leaves, coarsely torn

Halve each piece of French bread lengthwise. Melt the butter in a small saucepan, and stir in the chopped basil. Use this mixture to brush the cut sides of the bread. Bake the French bread in a preheated oven at 400°F for 4 minutes. Remove from the oven, and set aside while preparing the topping.

Peel and seed the tomatoes, and chop them coarsely. Place in a bowl, and add the diced mozzarella cheese. Season and mix well to combine. Spoon the tomato and mozzarella mixture evenly over the bread, and sprinkle with the Parmesan cheese. Drizzle a little olive oil over each pizza, and top with ground black pepper.

Return the pizzas to the oven, and bake for a further 10 minutes, until the topping is bubbling. Remove from the oven, and scatter basil leaves over the pizzas. Serve immediately.

MAKES FOUR SNACK PIZZAS

FRENCH BREAD PIZZA WITH GOAT CHEESE

4 tablespoons hazelnut oil
2 tablespoons sunflower oil
4 teaspoons chopped fresh thyme
4 slices French bread, cut on the diagonal
6 ounces zucchini
Salt and ground black pepper
10 ounces goat cheese
12 toasted hazelnuts, coarsely chopped
2 teaspoons fresh thyme leaves

Mix together the hazelnut oil, I tablespoon of the sunflower oil and the chopped thyme. Use this mixture to brush the cut sides of the French bread slices. Place the pieces of bread on a baking sheet, and bake in a preheated oven at 400°F for 5 minutes. Remove from the oven, and set aside while preparing the topping.

Cut the zucchini into julienne strips, and place in a bowl. Season the zucchini julienne well, and stir in the remaining sunflower oil. Slice the goat cheese into eight thin circles. Top each piece of French bread with a quarter of the zucchini julienne and two slices of goat cheese. Grind over some black pepper.

Return the pizzas to the oven, and bake for 6-8 minutes, until the cheese is bubbling. Remove the pizzas from the oven, and scatter with toasted hazelnuts and thyme leaves. Serve immediately.

MAKES FOUR SNACK PIZZAS

LEFT: French Bread Pizzas with Goat Cheese
RIGHT: French Bread Pizza Margherita

PUFF PASTRY PIZZA WITH ROASTED PEPPER & SALAMI

8-ounce package puff pastry
4 tablespoons Roasted Pepper Sauce (see page 14)
3 ounces Italian salami, in one thick piece
Ground black pepper
1 beaten egg
1 tablespoon snipped fresh chives

Roll out the puff pastry thinly on a lightly floured sur-face, and cut out six 2½-inch diamonds. Prick each pastry diamond with the prongs of a fork, and place them on a lightly greased baking sheet.

Spread the pepper sauce evenly between the six pastry diamonds, leaving a ¼-inch border around the edges. Cut the salami into ¼-inch cubes, and scatter these over the pepper sauce. Top each pizza with some ground black pepper. Brush the exposed edges of the puff pastry diamonds with the beaten egg.

Bake the pizzas in a preheated oven at 425°F for 7-8 minutes, until cooked through. Remove the pizzas from the oven, and sprinkle with the snipped chives. Serve immediately.   MAKES SIX SNACK PIZZAS

PUFF PASTRY PIZZA WITH LOX

8-ounce package puff pastry
1 beaten egg
¾ cup cream cheese
4 teaspoons milk
4 teaspoons lemon juice
Salt and ground black pepper
4 ounces lox
4 teaspoons snipped fresh chervil

Roll out the puff pastry thinly on a lightly floured sur-face, and cut out four 6-inch circles. Prick each pastry circle with the prongs of a fork, and place them on lightly greased baking sheets. Brush the circles with beaten egg, and bake them in a preheated oven at 425°F for 10 minutes.

Remove the pastry from the oven, and let cool slightly. Mix together the cream cheese, milk and lemon juice; season well. Spread the mixture evenly between the four pastry circles, leaving a ½-inch border around the edges. Slice the lox into thick strips, and arrange them evenly between the pizzas. Top with black pepper and the snipped chervil. Serve at once.   MAKES FOUR SNACK PIZZAS

RIGHT: Puff Pastry Pizzas with Lox

MUSHROOM FOCACCIA PIZZA

1 purchased focaccia bread
½ cup olive oil
4 cloves garlic, crushed
4 tablespoons chopped fresh mixed herbs, such as parsley, thyme and chives
¼ cup butter
10 ounces girolle mushrooms
Salt and ground black pepper

Cut the focaccia bread into six triangles. Mix 6 tablespoons of the olive oil with the crushed garlic and chopped herbs. Brush this mixture liberally all over the six focaccia triangles. Place the bread triangles on a baking sheet.

Wipe the mushrooms with damp paper towels, and slice any that are large. Heat the butter and the remaining oil in a large heavy-bottomed skillet. Add the prepared mushrooms, and sauté over a moderate heat for 4-5 minutes; season generously. Divide the mushrooms evenly over the six bread triangles.

Bake the pizzas in a preheated oven at 400°F for 7-10 minutes, until warmed through. Remove the pizzas from the oven, top with ground black pepper, and serve at once.   MAKES SIX SNACK PIZZAS

Variation: If you prefer, substitute a selection of wild mushrooms or cultivated mixed mushrooms, such as button, field and brown, for the girolle mushrooms in this recipe.

MARINARA FOCACCIA PIZZA

1 purchased focaccia bread
6 tablespoons extra virgin olive oil
4 cloves garlic, crushed
6 small plum tomatoes
6 black olives, pitted
Salt and ground black pepper
2 tablespoons chopped fresh oregano

Cut the focaccia bread into six triangles. Mix 4 tablespoons of the olive oil with the crushed garlic. Brush this mixture liberally all over the six focaccia triangles. Place the bread on a baking sheet.

Slice each tomato into three thick slices. Place three slices of tomato on each focaccia triangle. Slice the black olives into rings, and scatter these over the pizzas; season and drizzle on the remaining olive oil.

Bake the pizzas in a preheated oven at 400°F for 7-8 minutes, until the tomato slices have softened and the pizzas are warmed through. Remove from the oven, sprinkle with chopped oregano, and serve at once.

MAKES SIX SNACK PIZZAS

Variation: If you prefer, add slivered anchovies to these pizzas before baking them. Allow half an anchovy fillet per pizza triangle.

RIGHT: Mushroom Focaccia Pizza,
Marinara Focaccia Pizza

APRICOT & ALMOND DESSERT PIZZA

4 purchased 5-inch pizza bases
¼ cup melted butter

TOPPING

1 cup ground almonds
1 cup superfine sugar
2 egg yolks
¾ cup orange juice
48 dried apricots
4 tablespoons Amaretto liqueur
3 tablespoons apricot preserves

Make the almond topping. Mix together the ground almonds, superfine sugar, egg yolks and 4 tablespoons of the orange juice. Set aside.

Place the dried apricots in a saucepan with the remaining orange juice for about 15 minutes, until they are plump. Stir in the Amaretto liqueur, and simmer over a low heat for 4-5 minutes. Remove from the heat, and set aside.

Brush the pizza bases with the melted butter, and place them on baking sheets. Spread the almond topping evenly over the bases, leaving a ½-inch border around the edges. Drain the apricots, reserving liquid. Arrange twelve apricots over each pizza.

Bake the pizzas in a preheated oven at 400°F for 10-15 minutes, until cooked through.

Remove from the oven, and let cool slightly. Place the reserved liquid from the apricots in a small pan, add the apricot preserves, and simmer gently to dissolve the preserves. Brush the pizzas with the apricot glaze, and serve.   MAKES FOUR DESSERT PIZZAS

BANANA, RUM & RAISIN PIZZA

4 purchased 5-inch pizza bases
¼ cup melted butter
½ cup mascarpone cheese
Scant ½ cup dark rum
4 tablespoons brown sugar
3 tablespoons raisins
4 small bananas, sliced

Brush the pizza bases with half the melted butter, and place them on baking sheets. Bake the bases in a preheated oven at 400°F for 10-12 minutes, until pale golden. Remove from the oven, and set aside.

Mix the mascarpone cheese with 3 tablespoons of the rum, and spread the mixture evenly over the pizza bases, leaving a ½-inch border around the edges.

Place the remaining melted butter in a saucepan, add the remaining rum, brown sugar and raisins, and cook over a gentle heat for a few minutes, until the sugar has dissolved and the mixture is thick and syrupy. Add the sliced bananas, and mix through gently. Top each pizza with a quarter of the warm banana mixture, and serve at once.

MAKES FOUR DESSERT PIZZAS

TOP: Banana, Rum & Raisin Pizza
BOTTOM: Apricot & Almond Dessert Pizzas

APPLE & CINNAMON PUFF PASTRY PIZZA

10-ounce package puff pastry
Milk for brushing
Crème fraîche, to serve

APPLE PUREE

8 ounces eating apples, peeled, cored and diced
4 tablespoons water
3 tablespoons brown sugar
3 tablespoons Calvados
2 tablespoons unsalted butter

TOPPING

2 red-skinned apples
4 teaspoons brown sugar
1 teaspoon ground cinnamon

Roll out the pastry on a lightly floured surface, and cut out four dough rectangles measuring 6 x 4 inches. Place the rectangles on a baking sheet, prick them all over with a fork, and brush with a little milk. Bake in a preheated oven at 425°F for 10 minutes. Remove and reduce the temperature to 400°F.

Make the apple purée. Place the diced apple, water, sugar and Calvados in a small pan. Simmer the mixture gently for 10-15 minutes. Stir in the butter. Spread the apple purée evenly over the pastry rectangles, leaving a ½-inch border.

Make the topping. Slice the apples very thinly and arrange them over the apple purée. Mix together the brown sugar and cinnamon, and sprinkle over the apple slices. Return the pizzas to the oven, and bake for 5-8 minutes. Serve warm, accompanied by the crème fraîche.   MAKES FOUR DESSERT PIZZAS

CALZONE SORPRESA (CHOCOLATE CALZONE)

Basic Pizza Dough (see page 10)
Cornmeal for dusting
2 tablespoons melted butter
A little superfine sugar

FILLING

1¼ cups cream cheese
7 squares dark or milk chocolate
⅔ cup toasted hazelnuts
⅔ cup candied citrus peel

Prepare the dough as described in the basic recipe. While the dough is rising, make the filling.

Place the cream cheese in a bowl. Chop the chocolate and hazelnuts into small pieces, and add them to the cream cheese, together with the citrus peel. Mix until well combined.

When the dough is ready for use, divide it into five equal portions. Roll out each piece of dough to produce a 7-inch circle. Place one-fifth of the cream cheese mixture on one half of each dough circle. Dampen the edges of each circle with water, and fold over to produce five semi-circles. Seal the edges well. Place the calzones on baking sheets lightly dusted with cornmeal, and brush with melted butter. Sprinkle with a little superfine sugar.

Bake the calzones in a preheated oven at 475°F for 15 minutes, until crisp and golden. Remove from the oven, allow to cool slightly, and serve at once.

MAKES FIVE 7-INCH CALZONES

LEFT: Calzone Sorpresa
RIGHT: Apple & Cinnamon Puff Pastry Pizza

INDEX

American Hot Pizza 38
Anchovy, Broccoli and Pine Nut Pizza 22
Apple and Cinnamon Puff Pastry Pizza 78
Apricot and Almond Dessert Pizza 76
Avocado, Scamorza and Tomato Calzone 54

Banana, Rum and Raisin Pizza 76
Basic Pizza Dough 10
Basic Tomato Sauce 12
Blue Cheese, Bacon and Mushroom Pizza 24
Brie and Cherry Tomato Mini Pizzas 66

Calzone Caponata 50
Calzone Carbonara 52
Calzone Sorpresa 78
Checkerboard Pizza 68
Chicago-style Stuffed Pizza Pie 36
Chicken and Corn Calzone 50
Chili Con Carne Pizza 48
Chinese Chicken Pizza 42
Chocolate Calzone 78
Chorizo and Chickpea Pizza 42
Corn Sauce 16
Cornmeal Pizza Dough 10

Dessert pizzas 76, 78

Eggplant Pizzas 64
English Cheese Pizza 48
Equipment 8

Fennel Sfincione 62
French Bread Pizza Margherita 70
French Bread Pizza with Goat Cheese 70
Fresh Basil Pesto 16
Fresh Parsley Pesto 16
Fresh Tomato and Herb Sauce 12

Gorgonzola, Artichoke and Salami Sfincione 62
Greek-style Pizza 46

Ham, Pineapple and Corn Pizza 44

Italian Sausage and Leek Sfincione 60

Kneading pizza dough 6

Lamb Tikka Mini Pizzas 66

Marinara Focaccia Pizza 74
Mini pizzas 64, 66, 68

Mixed Mushroom Pizza 24
Mushroom Focaccia Pizza 74

Pestos 16
Pesto, Tomato and Garlic Pizza 26
Pissaladière Pizza 32
Pizza dough, preparation 6, 8, 10
Pizza Florentine 40
Pizza Frutti di Mare 22
Pizza Margherita 18
Pizza Napoletana 40
Pizza Niçoise 28
Pizza Parma 38
Pizza Pasticcio 44
Pizza Pescatore 46
Pizza Quattro Stagioni 30
Pizza Salumeria 34
Pizza Tre Pepperoni 20
Preparing pizzas 6, 8
Prosciutto and Fig Pizzas 64
Puff Pastry Pizza with Roasted Pepper
    and Salami 72
Puff Pastry Pizza with Lox 72
Puttanesca Pizza 32

Rich Pizza Dough 10
Roasted Garlic and Eggplant Pizza 20
Roasted Pepper Sauce 14

Salt Cod Calzone 58
Sauces 8, 12, 14, 16
Seafood Calzone 58
Sicilian Hot Pizza 34
Smoked Chicken and Parsley Pesto Pizza 26
Snack pizzas 70, 72, 74
Spicy Beef Calzone 54
Spinach and Pine Nut Calzone 56
Spring Vegetable Pizza 28
Storing dough 6
Sun-dried Tomato Pizza 18

Three-cheese Calzone 56
Tomato Sauce, Basic 12
Tomato and Chili Sauce 14
Tomato and Herb Sauce, Fresh 12

Vegetable Sfincione 60

Whole-wheat Pizza Dough 10

Zucchini and Smoked Ham Calzone 52